MONOLOGUES: MEN 2

50 SPEECHES FROM THE CONTEMPORARY THEATRE

ROBERT EMERSON
JANE GRUMBACH
EDITORS

DRAMA BOOK PUBLISHERS
NEW YORK

First Edition

 For information address
Drama Book Publishers, 821 Broadway,
New York, New York 10003.

LIBRARY OF CONGRESS CATALOGING IN PUBLICATION DATA

Main entry under title:

Monologues—men.

1. Acting. 2. Monologues. I. Emerson. Robert.
II. Grumbach, Jane.

PN2080.M55 822'.045 76-1027

ISBN 0-89676-065-0

Manufactured in the United States of America

CONTENTS

ACKNOWLEDGMENTS

From EQUUS by Peter Shaffer. Copyright (c) 1974 by Peter Shaffer. Reprinted by permission of Atheneum Publishers, Inc., from EQUUS AND SHRIVINGS by Peter Shaffer.

From EVERY GOOD BOY DESERVES FAVOR by Tom Stoppard. Copyright (c) 1978 by Tom Stoppard. Reprinted by permission of Grove Press, Inc.

From FANTASIES AT THE FRICK by Leonard Melfi. Copyright (c) 1980 by Leonard Melfi. Reprinted by permission of the author and Helen Harvey.

From FIND YOUR WAY HOME by John Hopkins. Copyright (c) 1975 (revised) by John Hopkins. Reprinted by permission of the author.

From GOOD EVENING by Peter Cook and Dudley Moore. Copyright (c) 1977 by Peter Cook and Dudley Moore. Reprinted by permission of the authors.

From THE GOODBYE PEOPLE by Herb Gardner. Copyright (c) 1974 by Herb Gardner. Reprinted by permission of Farrar, Straus and Giroux, Inc.

From GOTCHA by Barrie Keefe. Copyright (c) 1977 by Barrie Keefe. Reprinted by permission of Grove Press, Inc.

From HOSANNA by Michael Tremblay. Translation copyright (c) 1974 by John Van Burek and Bill Glassco. Reprinted by permission of Talonbooks Ltd.

From I WAS DANCING by Edwin O'Connor. Copyright (c) 1963 by Edwin O'Connor as an unpublished work. Copyright (c) 1966 by Edwin O'Connor. Reprinted by permission of Dramatists Play Service, Inc., and the author.

From JESSE AND THE BANDIT QUEEN by David Freeman. Copyright (c) 1976 by David Freeman. Reprinted by permission of International Creative Management.

From JOE EGG by Peter Nichols. Copyright (c) 1967 by Peter Nichols. Reprinted by permission of Grove Press, Inc.

From LEMON SKY by Lanford Wilson. Copyright (c) 1970 by Lanford Wilson. Reprinted by permission of Hill & Wang, a division of Farrar, Straus and Giroux, Inc.

From LOVERS by Brian Friel. Copyright (c) 1968 by Brian Friel. Reprinted by permission of International Creative Management.

From MY SWEET CHARLIE by David Westheimer. Copyright (c) 1967 by David Westheimer. Reprinted by permission of the author, Bob Banner Associates, and Samuel French, Inc.

From OF THE FIELDS, LATELY by David French. Copyright (c) 1975 by David French. Reprinted by permission of New Press, 30 Lesmill Road, Don Mills, Ontario, Canada.

From P.S. YOUR CAT IS DEAD! by James Kirkwood. Copyright (c) 1979 by Elyria Productions. Reprinted by permission of the author.

From PASSING GAME by Steve Tesich. Copyright (c) 1978 by Steve Tesich. Reprinted by permission of International Creative Management.

From PHILADELPHIA, HERE I COME by Brian Friel. Copyright (c) 1965 by Brian Friel. Reprinted by permission of International Creative Management.

From RED ROVER, RED ROVER by Oliver Hailey. Copyright (c) 1979 by Oliver Hailey. Reprinted by permission of the author and Paramuse Artists Associates.

From RICH AND FAMOUS by John Guare. Copyright (c) 1977 by St. Jude Productions, Inc. Reprinted by permission of the author.

From SAY GOODNIGHT, GRACIE by Ralph Pape. Copyright (c) 1979 by Ralph Pape. Reprinted by permission of the author.

From THE SEA HORSE by Edward J. Moore. Copyright (c) 1969, 1971, 1973, 1974 by Robert James Moore. Copyright (c) 1979 (revised and rewritten) by Robert James Moore. Reprinted by permission of James T. White and Co. and the author.

COMIC

BRINGING IT ALL BACK HOME by Terrence McNally

Jimmy -- 20 MALE -- COMIC

A soldier killed in Vietnam remembers his life and death.

(Sitting up.) Well here's Jimmy. Here he is. (Flashes a smile.) Dad's making one of his obscene phone calls. This might be my only chance to talk. I'm really dead, you understand, but I can clear the air up a little bit. At least get the facts straight. I'm six foot one . . . was, I was six foot one, sorry about that . . . weighed one fifty-nine, had blue eyes and hair the color commonly called dirty blonde. Now don't feel too badly that they didn't remember all that. I couldn't answer the same questions about any of them. I mean jeez, I'm just their son and brother! But I can't understand half the things they've said about me. Like Susy. How can you call someone a good big brother when he took a brick and knocked your permanent front teeth out? That's a bridge she's flashing. Johnny's decided I was a load of laughs. What's an Italian pushing a baby carriage? That's the only joke I can remember, and even so I forget the punch line. And like everybody else I must have heard hundreds, thousands of jokes in my lifetime. I just never could remember them. And God only knows I never made one up. Dad's decided I was masculine all of a sudden and mom's gnawing the patriotism bone. I swear I don't know who they're talking about. And that bit about he never knew what hit him! At first I was just startled, I mean I never expected it to happen to me, but after a minute or two it hurt like hell. You have your guts hanging out and see how it feels! I'm sorry. I'm not meant to show any emotion. I'm dead. Thank you for your attention. . . . Is anybody wondering how it feels to be dead? I'll try to tell you. It's a . . . funny feeling. Funny because it's so hard to talk about. You see, there I was just kind of slopping around and I'd never really thought about what being alive meant and so now it's kind of hard to compare the two. But when I stepped on that mine I knew something had hit me. I can tell you that! Christ Almighty, it hurt! (Flashes a smile.) Well here goes Jimmy. Here he goes. (He signals the peace sign and lies back down.)

WHERE HAS TOMMY FLOWERS GONE? by Terrence McNally

Arnold -- an ageless dog MALE -- COMIC

A dog finds man's behavior amusing.

I didn't always have Tommy Flowers and I'm not at all sure I always will. I got him when I was given back to him by a friend of his who didn't want me after Tommy had given me to him in the first place. It's complicated, I know. This friend was a very lonely sort of person and Tommy decided that he should have a dog. Only he didn't want a dog. But when he saw me something inside of him must have snapped because his eyes kind of filled up like he was going to cry and he held me very close. I was this big then! And he didn't say anything and he walked a few feet away from everyone and stood with his back to them and just held me like a little baby. No one had to ask if he wanted me. You could just tell. I was so happy. But the next morning he didn't want me at all. There I was, just kind of slumped in my box, all droopy-eyed and warm nosed and not looking at all too hot. Puppy chill is all it was. Tommy said they'd just take me to the vet but the friend didn't want a sick dog. He didn't want any dog. And you know what his reason was? They die on you. That's what he said. They die on you. We do, you know. Everything does. But is that a reason? How could anyone not want me? Oh, don't get any ideas. I'm not a talking dog. I'm a thinking one. There's a difference!

SEXUAL PERVERSITY IN CHICAGO by David Mamet

Bernard -- 20s MALE -- COMIC

Bernard relates his latest conquest.

But the shot is, while we're fucking, she wants me, every thirty seconds or so, to go BOOM at the top of my lungs. So we're humping and bumping and greasing the old Flak suit and every once in a while I go BOOM, and she starts in on me. "Turn me over," she says, so I do. She's on her stomach. I'm on top . . . So she's on her stomach, et cetera. In the middle of everything she slithers over to the side of the bed, picks up the house phone and says "Give me Room 511." "Who are you calling?" I say. "A friend," she says. So okay. They answer the phone. "Patrice," she says, "It's me, I'm up here with a friend, and I could use a little help. Could you help me out?" So all of a sudden I hear coming out of the phone: "Rat Tat Tat Tat Tat. Ka POW! AK AK AK AK AK AK AK Ka Pow!" So fine. I'm pumping away, the chick on the other end is making airplane noises, every once in a while I go BOOM, and the broad on the bed starts going crazy. She's moaning and groaning and about to go the whole long route. Humping and bumping, and she's screaming "Red dog One to Red dog Squadron" . . . all of a sudden she screams "Wait." She wriggles out, leans under the bed, and she pulls out this five-gallon jerrycan. . . . Opens it up . . . it's full of gasoline. So she splashes the mother all over the walls, whips a fuckin' Zippo out of the Flak suit, and WHOOSH, the whole room is in flames. So the whole fuckin' joint is going up in smoke, the telephone is going "Rat Tat Tat," the broad jumps back on the bed and yells "Now, give it to me now for the Love of Christ." (Pause.) So I look at the broad . . . and I figure . . . fuck this nonsense. I grab my clothes, I peel a sawbuck off my wad, as I make the door I fling it at her. "For cabfare," I yell. She doesn't hear nothing. One, two, six, I'm in the hall. Struggling into my shorts and hustling for the elevator. Whole fucking hall is full of smoke, above the flames I just make out my broad (she's singing "Off We Go into the Wild

Blue Yonder"), and the elevator arrives, and the whole fucking hall is full of firemen. (Pause.) Those fucking firemen make out like bandits.

THE TRIP BACK DOWN by John Bishop

Chuck -- 24 MALE -- COMIC

A young man tells of the first time he saw his hero race.

I was so excited I had to pee as soon as we got through the gate. And that, of course, pissed my old man off incredibly. "Whyn't you think of that before we left home?" he said. As if a kid goes around thinkin' about whether or not he's gotta pee. We sat high in the stands on the fourth turn, and comes the main race and somebody in the group puts money on you. My old man says, "Shit, he's just a punk kid. He's nobody. He's lucky if he finishes the race." And then . . . right then . . . I began to root for ya. Under my breath, of course, but I began to root. And pray. "Please, God," I said, "let the punk kid win this race. Let this fat son of a bitch next to me not always be right." 'Course I don't think I said son of a bitch. Not to God. But I rooted. "C'mon, Bob," I said to myself. "C'mon, number 14." And you started to catch up. Somebody yelled, "That Bobby Horvath is drivin' like a crazy man." And then on the inside groove at the far turn you got underneath the second car and right in front of me you took him. Christ, right in front of me. The crowd was suddenly on their feet screaming. It was you and the leader now . . . number 33.

I jumped up on my seat to see better. You were right up to the leader . . . and somebody yelled, "Goddamn you, Bobby, go and get him!" The white flag came out. One lap. You got one lap. And then, at the far end of the track you caught the leader. You caught that son of a bitch. I screamed out loud, "C'mon, Bobby!" And I think my old man about shit! I could feel him lookin' at me but I didn't care anymore. 'Cause you was up to the leader. Draftin' him right off his left rear, bangin' his tail . . . pressin' harder than you should . . . pushin' him more than he wanted to be pushed . . . blastin' into the third turn . . . firin' down the straightaway . . . then up next to him on the outside . . . the two of you comin' into the finish like you was glued together . . . I screamed, I yelled, I promised God I'd go to Sunday School and quit jackin' off . . . and they slammed that checkered flag down on you! Man, what a race.

RICH AND FAMOUS by John Guare

Tybalt -- 20s MALE -- COMIC

An actor has his future all planned out.

After Gangland I got all these offers. I said to my lawyers and my agents as a joke really -- I said it's a shame I have to go and try to top Gangland. I'm a legend now. I don't want to do any parts that'll hurt my legend. Protect myself. Lucky Jimmy Dean. Lucky Marilyn. Lucky people like that. Jesus. Lucky Jesus. Never get old. No work. No sweat. No reality getting in the way of my immortality. The lawyers and the agents looked at each other. As a matter of fact, Kid, we were thinking of approaching you. It can be arranged. . . .

My death. . . . I'll be a multi-million dollar industry. I've posed for nude photos that'll be released in a year. I've written, had written for me, a beautiful book with all my hopes and dreams. I wish I'd known you wanted to be a writer. You could have done some of my ghost work. I've shot scenes that are going to be inserted into Marilyn's old movies so we can seem to appear together. They think we'll make a great team. They're making a movie of my life. Cameras hidden down there filming my leap. Norman then is doing a beautiful, has done it already, picture book, you know, for coffee tables, a book of my life and death and why. Why. That's the title. Then they'll make a play out of it. Then a movie version. Then a stage musical of the movie. Then a movie musical of my life. Then a TV series. Then a spinoff. They'll be looking for someone to play me. They'll be starting a major search to find me. Maybe you could go up. Audition. I could give you the names of the top people in the industry to see. Or maybe you could write my life and sell it to the magazines. The small ones. The big mags have already been contracted. The early Tyb. I hadn't planned on that. God, I wish I had known you wanted to be a writer. That you found that little store on Fourteenth Street. That you wore the cufflinks. Just before I came up here, I went back to Fourteenth Street. Returned the cufflinks. Let somebody else use them. Tybalt's boyhood. We had fun, didn't we? Did we? I can't remember. I always thought about the future so much, I never remembered the past. I wanted to be rich and famous so badly. But we're afraid to grow. I was so afraid to take the plunge into immortality. To settle for the old rich and famous. I'll never have to work again. The most returns for the least outlay. No sweat. I'm lucky. Always have been lucky. No strings. No ties.

TABLE MANNERS by Alan Ayckbourn

Norman -- 30s, English MALE -- COMIC

Having failed in an attempt to carry off his wife's sister for an illicit weekend, Norman faces a group of hostile in-laws at breakfast.

Nothing wrong in a few drinks. Don't speak. I don't care. Going to be a pretty dull Sunday if we all sit in silence, I can tell you. Well, I'm not sitting in silence. I'll find something to do. I know, I'll go up and frighten Mother. . . . Ah-ha! Nearly got you again. Is it too much to ask for something to eat? (No response.) It's too much to ask for something to eat. May I borrow your bowl? That's awfully nice of you. And your spoon? Thank you. Now then, what shall I have? Puffa Puffa rice. Ah-ha . . . No Sunday papers. Dear, dear. Ah, well I shall have to read my morning cereal

. . . (<u>He laughs.</u>) Cereal. Do we all get that? Apparently we don't. (<u>He reads.</u>) Stop! Stop everything. Listen. A free pair of pinking shears for only 79p and six Puffa Puffa tokens. Hurry, hurry, hurry. What's this? Is nobody hurrying? Do you mean to tell me that none of you want them? Where's the spirit of British pinking? Dead, presumably. Like my relations. Hang on, I've got another game. Mind reading. I'll read your minds. Now then, where shall we start? Sarah. Sarah is thinking -- that noisy man up there should be home with his wife. What is he doing shattering the calm of our peaceful Sunday breakfast with his offers of reduced price pinking shears? Why is he here, shouting at us like this? Why isn't he at home, like any other decent husband, shouting at his wife? He came down here to seduce his wife's own sister. How low can he get? The fact that his wife's own sister said, at one stage anyway, that she was perfectly happy to go along with him is beside the point. The fact that little Annie here was perfectly happy to ditch old reliable Tom -- without a second thought -- and come off with me is beside the point. We won't mention that because it doesn't quite fit in with the facts as we would like them. And what is little Annie thinking, I wonder? Maybe furtively admiring my pyjamas, who knows? Pyjamas that could have been hers. With all that they contain. These nearly were mine. Or maybe she is thinking . . . Phew, that was a close shave. I could have been shacked up in some dreadful hotel with this man -- at this very moment . . . what a lucky escape for me. Thank heavens, I am back here at home amidst my talkative family exchanging witty breakfast banter. Knowing my two-legged faithful companion and friend, Tom the rambling vet, is even now planning to propose to me in 1997 just as soon as he's cured our cat. Meanwhile, I can live here peacefully, totally fulfilled, racing up and down stairs looking after Mother, having the time of my life and living happily ever after until I'm fifty-five and fat . . . I'm glad I didn't go to that hotel. Well, let me tell you so am I. I wouldn't want a weekend with you, anyway. And I'll tell you the funniest thing of all, shall I? . . . I didn't even book the hotel. I knew you wouldn't come. You didn't have the guts.

JESSE AND THE BANDIT QUEEN by David Freeman

Jesse -- 30s

MALE -- COMIC

<u>The famous outlaw explains the events surrounding his death.</u>

Sixteen years of making history and little Bobby Ford was the best they could do. All them Pinkerton men with their squads and staffs and long guns and little Bobby Ford was the winner. What the hell do I care about pictures on a wall. I was dusting it or straightening it or some damn thing. Zee was cooking and getting ready for the Howards to go to Church. That was our name, Howard. Zee was always worried I'd get arrested if people knew our name. Course we had monogrammed everything. J. J. sewn into every damn thing in the house. Bobby Ford. He used to work for me. Nice kid. Stupid.

I never believed that story about the governor paying him $10,000 or whatever. How the hell would that pimply faced dodo ever even meet the governor let alone make a deal with him. I always thought what he wanted was to get his sneaky little hands on my wife's ass. I was the same way with Belle when I was his age. Hell, when I got older too. Couldn't keep my hands off her from the day I met her.

EVERY GOOD BOY DESERVES FAVOR by Tom Stoppard

Alexander -- 30s MALE -- COMIC

<u>A political prisoner relates a friend's troubles with the authorities.</u>

One day they arrested a friend of mine for possessing a controversial book, and they kept him in mental hospitals for a year and a half. I thought this was an odd thing to do. Soon after he got out, they arrested a couple of writers, A and B, who had published some stories under different names. Under their own names they got five years and seven years hard labor. I thought this was most peculiar. My friend, C, demonstrated against the arrest of A and B. I told him he was crazy to do it, and they put him back into the mental hospital. D was a man who wrote to various people about the trial of A and B and held meetings with his friends E, F, G, and H, who were all arrested, so I, J, K, L, and a fifth man demonstrated against the arrest of E, F, G, and H, and were themselves arrested. D was arrested the next day. The fifth man was my friend C, who had just got out of the mental hospital where they put him for demonstrating against the arrest of A and B, and I told him he was crazy to demonstrate against the arrest of E, F, G, and H, and he got three years in a labor camp. I thought this really wasn't fair. M compiled a book on the trials of C, I, J, K, and L, and with his colleagues N, O, P, Q, R, and S attended the trial of T who had written a book about his experiences in a labor camp, and who got a year in a labor camp. This trial took place on August the twenty-first of 1968, and in the courtroom it was learned that the Russian army had gone to the aid of Czechoslovakia. M, N, O, P, Q, R, and S decided to demonstrate in Red Square the following Sunday, when they were all arrested and variously disposed of in labor camps, psychiatric hospitals, and internal exile. Three years had passed since the arrest of A and B. C finished his sentence about the same time as A and then he did something really crazy. He started telling everybody that sane people were being put in mental hospitals for their political opinions. By the time B finished his sentence, C was on trial for anti-Soviet agitation and slander, and he got seven years in prison and labor camps, and five years exile . . . You see all the trouble writers cause.

WHISKEY by Terrence McNally

Johnny -- mid 30s MALE -- COMIC

An ex-quarterback is sick of the insinuation that he is gay.

Goddamnit, I'm gonna pull this trigger if I hear that word again. Faggot? Faggot? I grew up in Waco and I was punching girls 'fore my daddy let me have my learner's permit to drive our pickup. I had their panties off and I was in there, and I don't mean with my finger, 'fore most guys' balls had even dropped! Shit, the only faggots in Waco was punched-up, beat-up and stomped-on faggots. And me and my boys did the punching and the beating and the stomping. Goddamnit, I went to Texas A&M! That's a military school. Did you ever hear of a faggot from Texas A&M? From any military school for that matter? Hell, a place like that's so goddamned screened you can't get near the place if your big toe looks a little queer to 'em. Boy, my blood is boiling. Boy, you're getting my goat. I know the CIA is listening to every goddamn word I'm saying. Jesus H. Christ. I was a goddamn football star. We beat Texas three years running when I was on varsity. We was conference champs. I was quarterback. Did you ever hear of a gay quarterback? A cheerleader maybe, but I'll give you $500 for every gay quarterback you can name. All right, I know gay's one of them "in" words. I know it don't mean happy. But goddamn it to hell anyway! I'm in show business. I meet people. I hear how they talk. I admit it. There are certain people of the homosexual persuasion in my profession . . . All right, I'll admit this, too, only it's the first and last time I'm ever gonna say it clear out. There was a pansy at Texas A&M. Just one. But he wasn't in the corps. He was in animal husbandry. Now I didn't know him personally but I heard he was a damn nice guy from Tyler. 'Course when we found out he was a pansy we stomped the shit out o' him. My four years at Texas A&M were the happiest and proudest of my life. And if you don't think I fucked every weekend, then you're way off base. Hell, those College Townies drop their drawers and flop over backwards at the first sight o' field boots. A&M cadets could get laid in a goddamn convent, that's the kind of studs they are. And me being voted Most Valuable Player of the Southwest Conference three times in a row didn't exactly hurt none either. I got laid so much at A&M I landed up in the infirmary every spring semester with sexual hyperthesia.

YANKS 3 DETROIT 0 TOP OF THE SEVENTH by Jonathan Reynolds

Duke -- 36 MALE -- COMIC

Standing on the mound while pitching a no-hitter, a ball-player worries about his future.

I don't believe it. Old Salt? Old Saltine. That man lives for one thing: his obituary. Just keeps pumpin' out those quotes. Sooner or later he's bound to hit the right one -- and then there'll be nobody around to take it down. Boy, was he furious when Vince Lombardi died first. Now he's just staying alive to put some distance between the two legends. If he was smart, he'd kick off this afternoon before anyone finds out what a goon he is. YANKEE MANAGER DIES AT 65 OF EXCESS WISDOM. NATION MOURNS LOSS. PRESIDENT EXTOLS VIRTUES: "TO THE BEST OF MY KNOWLEDGE, OLD SALT NEVER URINATED IN HIS ENTIRE LIFE -- AN EXAMPLE, ONE OF MANY GOOD ONES, FOR THE YOUTH OF AMERICA." (He yells to the umpire offstage.) Hey! Can I throw a couple? (He quickly throws two pitches, each time limbering up his bruised shoulder.) I know this sounds silly, but whenever he does that "I have confidence" routine, I actually feel a lot better. Some of the brambles get cleared away. But it doesn't last. Lookit this team. I never felt so insecure in my life. If it hadn't been for those back-to-back homers by Popeye and Bruno in the second, I'd be in the toilet already. They came through. Not like my coconut buddy at Third. Lookit him. All he does is flash his gums and say, "I'ng no Paneech, I'ng Coob'n." Lookit him? Lookit me -- I just dove after that Nazi's grounder like a fag was after my boy Mitch. I could've dislocated my shoulder! Oh, this is a dopey game. (The ball comes back.) There's no strategy in baseball. You know what the strategy is in baseball? When you got a right-handed pitcher, you put up a left-handed batter; when you got a left-handed pitcher, you put up a right-handed batter. That's it. That's all the strategy there is. I used to be so excited with all this, but I'm not anymore. I'm excited . . . but I'm also bored. I'm bored with the excitement. When I first came up, whew, when I was doin' good, this game meant everything to me. I could lick anyone. Now it's just bases . . . changin' clothes . . . fake dirt . . . 20,000 paid and furious fans dyin' for me to fail. I just don't have the confidence to know what to do next. Look: Suppose your career's over -- what're ya gonna do? (Pause.) I don't know. Breathe. I'm gonna lose Donna Luna Donna, that's for sure. She's outside in m'66 Lincoln right now, listenin' to the game on the radio, and protectin' my hubcaps from the Cuban's cousins. She's my Texas groupie, and I think about her all the time. What I like best about her is her body. What she likes best about me is that I'm famous. C'mon, c'mon, back to business, back to business.

P.S. YOUR CAT IS DEAD! by James Kirkwood

Jimmy -- 38 MALE -- COMIC

An actor thinks he may have chosen the wrong profession.

You should have caught me auditioning for a TV commercial last week. Now get this scene: nine men and three women glued together behind this long conference table, staring at me like they're producing "War and Peace meets Ben Hur!" instead of a one-minute commercial for some new soft drink. "Squirt/Splash/Squat/Snatch," something momentous like that. (Giggles.) Catch the director: (Very pompous.) "Mr. Zoole? -- Zoole, is that -- ah -- your real name?" No -- like I changed it for the stage, right? (Then.)

"Yes it's my real name." (The director again.) "Mr. Zoole, here's our scene: You dive into a pool, swim the length, jump out, shake off the water, and our spokeswoman hands you the drink. You take a sip and say, "Wow, that's the most refreshing -- what is it?" Only one line, but it's important. Think you can handle that?" Well, I don't know, I've only been in the business twenty years. Maybe I should start out with something simple like: "Da-da, goo-goo, kah-kah!" "Yes, I think I can handle that." (Back to the director.) "Okay, Mr. Zoole, dive in!" Dive in! He actually wants me to dive in. (Dives in and pantomimes swimming from up left to down right.) And I swim the length of the conference table. Up, out, shake it off. (Shakes off imaginary water.) And I'm just reaching up for this non-existent can when the director says, "Wait-a-minute, Mr. Zoole, you didn't look as if you were enjoying the swim!" Oh, Christ, how I wanted to say: "No, you see, there was a little speck of shit in the pool -- you!" But, see -- You want the job. You want it so badly that -- glamorous! I got a million of 'em. I got a humiliation a minute. I got a humiliation a lifetime. I'm so tired of being charming and nice to everyone.

THIEVES by Herb Gardner

Martin -- 40 MALE -- COMIC

A husband is somewhat bewildered by his wife's behavior.

First, Sally . . . First I want you to know how much I appreciate the wonderful work you've done on our apartment here. How you've managed to capture, in only five short weeks, the subtle elusive, yet classic mood previously found only in the Port Authority Bus Terminal. (Pacing about the room.) In addition, Sally, you have, somewhat mystically, lost or forgotten the name of the moving and storage company with whom you placed nearly fifty-five thousand dollars worth of our furniture. . . . This, coupled with the fact that you disappeared eight days ago on what was ostensibly a trip to Gristede Brothers to buy some strawberry yogurt, and did not return until this evening, has led to a certain amount of confusion for me . . . (Opens crumpled letter.) All confusion, of course, vanished with the arrival last week of this simple, touching, yet concise note from the Misters Morris, Klien, Fishback and Fishback . . . (Reads, only the slightest tremor in his voice.) "We have been retained by your wife, Sally Jane Cramer, hereinafter referred to as 'Wife,' to represent her in the matter of your divorce. Said wife having requested that her whereabouts remain unknown to you at present, we therefore . . ." (Carefully folding letter into paper airplane.) After eight days of staring into the air-conditioner, wondering which Santini Brother had my furniture, which Gristede Brother had my wife, and which Fishback owned my soul, a light began to dawn . . . or maybe one went out . . . and I realized that nobody was hiding you from me, that your whereabouts, said wife, have been unknown to me for years . . . that you make a fine letter-writer, a great decorator, and a perfect stranger. You said you came back tonight to talk about the divorce. You didn't mention it. Neither did I. And the habit, the habit of being together, began again. But I couldn't sleep. I couldn't sleep and I thought about it and tonight, Sally, I have decided to retire from the games. The Olympics are over, lady, the torch is out . . . and you are free. (He tosses the paper airplane.) Said husband, hereinafter referred as "gone," has had it.

TALLEY'S FOLLY by Lanford Wilson

Matt -- 42, German-Jewish MALE -- COMIC

Matt introduces the audience to the setting of the play.

They tell me that we have ninety-seven minutes here tonight -- without intermission. So if that means anything to anybody; if you think you'll need a drink of water or anything . . .

You know, a year ago I drove Sally home from a dance; and while we were standing on the porch up at the house, we looked down to the river and saw this silver flying thing rise straight up and zip off. We came running down to the river, we thought the Japanese had landed some amazing new flying machine, but all we found was the boathouse here, and -- uh, that was enough.

I'll just point out some of the facilities till everybody gets settled in. If everything goes well for me tonight, this should be a waltz, one-two-three, one-two-three; a no-holds-barred romantic story, and since I'm not a romantic type, I'm going to need the whole valentine here to help me: the woods, the willows, the vines, the moonlight, the band -- there's a band that plays tonight, over in the park. The trees, the berries, the breeze, the sounds: water and crickets, frogs, dogs, the light, the bees, working all night.

Did you know that? Bees work -- worker bees -- work around the clock. Never stop. Collecting nectar, or pollen, whatever a bee collects. Of course their life expectancy is twenty days. Or, in a bee's case, twenty days and twenty nights. Or possibly "expectancy" is wrong in the case of a bee. Who knows what a bee expects. But whatever time there is in a life is a lifetime, and I imagine after twenty days and twenty nights a bee is more or less ready to tuck it in.

(In a craggy, Western, "Old-Timer" voice.) "I been flyin' now, young sprout, nigh-on to nineteen days an' nineteen nights."

(Imitating a young bee.) "Really, Grandpa Worker Bee?"

(Old-Timer.) "An' I'm 'bout ready to tuck it in."

(Slight pause. Reflectively.) Work. Work is very much to the point. (Showing the set.) We have everything to help me here. There's a rotating gismo in the footlights (do you believe footlights) because we needed the moon out there on the water. The water runs right through here, so you're all out in the river -- sorry about that. They promise me moonlight by the baleful, all through the shutters. We could do it on a couple of folding chairs, but it isn't bare, it isn't bombed out, it's run-down, and the difference is all the difference. And valentines need frou-frou.

We have a genuine Victorian folly here. A boathouse. Constructed of louvers, and lattice and geegaws. I feel like a real-estate salesman. Of course there's something about the term "real estate" that strikes me as wrong. Estate maybe, but real is arguable. But to start you off on the right foot . . . Everybody ready? This is a waltz, remember, one-two-three, one-two-three.

GOOD EVENING by Peter Cook and Dudley Moore

Dudley -- middle-aged MALE -- COMIC

A father has the sad task of explaining his wife's death to their son.

Roger, here is your Mother's signet ring she wanted you to have and wear for her. Took me two hours to get it off her bloody finger. And if you wouldn't mind wearing this black armband in memory of your Mother. I know she'd be pleased because she sewed it especially for you. . . . Roger, your Mother left this life as she lived it, screaming her bloody head off. I remember it very well, it was a Wednesday afternoon. Uncle Ralph had come in for a cup of tea, we hadn't seen him for twenty years and we were, you know, talking about when we used to walk over the cliffs at Leigh on Sea watching the boats come in -- he's a boring bugger, that Ralph -- once every twenty years is good enough for me. Anyway, Mother was lying very quietly, very still, almost at rest and suddenly, without a word of a lie, she sat bolt upright in bed, she went, "Aargh" (Screams.) her false teeth hit the ceiling and that was it. Your Mother never did anything by halves -- both sets -- POW -- hit the electric light bulb, the bulb fell to the floor, smashed, matron came running in, slipped on the broken glass, hit her head on the bedpost, killed outright . . . Nurse Oviatt, hearing the commotion, came roaring in from the President Roosevelt Memorial Ward, tripped over matron and went flying out the window. She fell five stories onto a car that was coming into the forecourt. It was an open car, she killed herself and the two passengers. The weight of the three dead bodies on the accelerator took that car roaring into the catering department, killed seven nurses, knocked ten orderlies into a huge vat of boiling potatoes. Well naturally, the valve on the vat got stuck and there was a tremendous explosion -- and the first floor collapsed. Well you can imagine what that did to the second and third floors. Anyway, son, I won't bore you with details -- suffice it to say, that I was the sole survivor. Nine hundred and eighty-seven people wiped out in a flash of your Mother's teeth.

LOVERS by Brian Friel

Andy -- 50, Irish MALE -- COMIC

In trying to gain the upper hand over his mother-in-law, Andy has shown her an article declaring her patron saint invalidated by the Pope.

I don't think I told you about the tenant I have over in Riverview. Retired accountant. Quiet couple. No kids. He pays me on the first Saturday of every month. Sometimes if the weather's good I take an odd walk over there and look at the outside of the house. He has rose trees in the front and vegetables at the back. Very nice. Very cozy. But by the time you get home from work and get washed you don't feel like going out much. So I usually sleep at the fire for a while and then come out here for a breath of air. Kills an hour or two. And then when the bell rings I go up to the aul woman's room for prayers. Well, I mean to say, anything for a quiet life. Hanna sleeps there now, as a matter of fact, just in case the aul woman should get an attack during the night. Not that that's likely. The doctor says she'll go on forever.

And a funny thing, you know, nothing much has changed up there. Philomena's gone, of course. But she still has the altar and she still lights the candles and has the flowers in the middle and she still faces it when she's praying and mouths away to it. I says to Cissy one night I says, "Who's she supposed to be praying to?" "A saint," says she very quick. "What saint?" says I, "Sure there's no statue there." "I'm not blind," says she. "Well, I mean to say," says I, "what does she think she's at?" "True enough, there's no statue there," says Cissy, "but we have a saint in our mind when we're praying even though we have no figure for it." "What saint?" says I. "Aha!" says she, "That's something you'll never know! Wild horses wouldn't drag that out of us. You robbed her of Saint Philomena but you'll never be told who it is!"

Crafty, eh? And when I go into the bedroom she smiles and nods at me and you can see her lips saying "Thank you thank you," to the altar. And when we kneel down, she says, "It's so nice for me to have you all gathered around my bed." As a certain American cleric says, "The family that prays together stays together." By God, you've got to admire the aul bitch. She could handle a regiment.

THE DOCK BRIEF by John Mortimer

Morgenhall -- 60s, English MALE -- COMIC

A less than competent lawyer relives the agony of his defense of a man who killed his wife.

He's not here at the moment -- he's not. . . .? Oh, I'm so glad. Just out temporarily? With the governor? Then, I'll wait for him. Poor soul. How's he taking it? You're not allowed to answer questions? The regulations, I suppose. Well, you must obey the regulations. I'll just sit down here and wait for Mr. Fowle. (He whistles. Whistling stops.) May it please you, my Lord, members of the jury. I should have said, may it please you, my Lord, members of the jury. I should have said . . . (He begins to walk up and down.) Members of the jury. Is there one of you who doesn't crave for peace . . . crave for peace. The silence of an undisturbed life, the dignity of an existence without dependents . . . without jokes. Have you never been tempted? . . . I should have said . . . Members of the jury. You and I are men of the world. If your Lordship would kindly not interrupt my speech to the jury. I'm obliged. Members of the jury, before I was so rudely interrupted. . . . I might have said . . . Look at the prisoner, members of the jury. Has he hurt you, done you the slightest harm? Is he not the mildest of men? He merely took it upon himself to regulate his domestic affairs. An Englishman's home is his castle. Do any of you feel a primitive urge, members of the jury, to be revenged on this gentle bird fancier . . . Members of the jury, I see I'm affecting your emotions but let us consider the weight of the evidence . . . I might have said that! I might have said . . . (With distress.) I might have said something. . . .

THE GOODBYE PEOPLE by Herb Gardner

Marcus -- 72 MALE -- COMIC

An old man has had enough of the rat race.

Listen to you! Max, I don't see you now a long time because you make me nervous! Always excited and you holler too much! Three years ago, the hurricane; I come around here the next day, I'm hoping this place would blow away. The sea should come and get it, it wouldn't aggravate me any more. You gather me? But it didn't blow away and neither do you! You're still around hollering and you make me nervous, Silverman . . . Take my advice, I come to tell you personally: be an old man, you'll live longer . . . Max, listen to me . . . this year I started doing old-man things. I tell stories for a second time, just like an old man. Sometimes for a third time. It's coming out of my mouth about how I got a good buy on my new car, the third time I'm telling it to my daughter and her husband. I know it's the third time, but I go right on, it doesn't bother me; just like an old man. I fall asleep in front of people like it's my right and my privilege, just like an old man. I can remember what I did, what clothes I wore, names of people from when I was eighteen, and if you told me I was in Hong Kong yesterday, I would believe you, because I don't remember; just like an old man. So, I finally figured it out. The reason I'm behaving like an old man . . . is because I'm an old man. A revelation to me, Silverman; and for the first time in years I'm not annoyed with myself. Silverman, I was not a top businessman. I was good, but not first-class. I was an O.K. husband; and as a father, not a knockout. But, Max . . . I'm a great old man. I do that the best. I was born for it. I'm seventy-two, Max, and it fits me like a glove. You, you're crazy. I wish you well with the business, but I can't join you . . . (He smiles.) See, I'm too old for it.

SERIOUS

GOTCHA by Barrie Keefe

Kid -- 16, English MALE -- SERIOUS

Holding 3 teachers hostage, a student berates them for their indifference.

I could see it . . . in your eyes . . . I can see what you think. It's in your eyes . . . First day here . . . lined up in front of you, all hundreds of us -- the new kids. Lined up in the playground . . . all of us in lines and you wandering along, eyes flickering over us . . . deciding who's doing what, who's going where. Flick of the eyes . . . he's got a nice jacket. Clean trousers and starched handkerchief . . . O levels for him. Like Party says, you see the no-hopers . . . relegate them. Out of the way. (He takes a long drag on his cigarette.) Listen to your chat, speech-day -- mayor there . . . talking. About how proud he is of this school, this everso terrific comprehensive school . . . the big, big, school . . . everyone all together . . . all chances, hundreds of subjects, something for everyone, put out your hand and take what you want -- But . . . watched your eyes . . . not even looking at the poor sod of a mayor. "Humour him," your eyes said. "Humour him. Dreamer!" (He sighs. Pause.) Now . . . found out . . . I was right. Comprehensive! (He spits.) Me brother, me brother, wow, what he said about it when I come here! Chance for you, kiddo, he said to me. Secondary school he went to. No hope. Chucked in there. Factory fodder, but this comprehensive! Paradise. So different he said . . . and he supposed to know. Knows the mayor, delivered his leaflets for him at elections, me brother did. Knew all about what was gonna happen in this new school. This is your big chance, kiddo, he says . . . (Pause.) Got it wrong. Just the same. Only bigger. Anything you want here, they said. Yeah. If you're clever, if you're bright, big hope . . . glittering prizes! Just the same, as it was for me brother . . . just . . . the same. Only bigger. Achievement successes . . . only way it's judged . . . all them O levels, all them A levels, all them clever bastards going to university. What a clever headmaster, what a smashing lot of teachers, what a great school. What a fantastic school -- What about us? Who don't do O levels? What about me, eh?

EQUUS by Peter Shaffer

Alan -- 17, English MALE -- SERIOUS

A boy guilty of blinding 6 horses tells his psychiatrist how his obsession with the animal began.

That's what you want to know, isn't it? All right: it was. I'm talking about the beach. That time when I was a kid. What I told you about . . . I was pushed forward on the horse. There was sweat on my legs from his neck. The fellow held me tight, and let me turn the horse which way I wanted.

All that power going any way you wanted . . . His sides were all warm, and the smell . . . Then suddenly I was on the ground, where Dad pulled me. I could have bashed him . . . (Pause.) Something else. When the horse first appeared, I looked up into his mouth. It was huge. There was this chain in it. The fellow pulled it, and cream dripped out. I said "Does it hurt?" And he said -- the horse said -- said (He stops in anguish. Desperately.) It was always the same, after that. Every time I heard one clop by, I had to run and see. Up a country lane or anywhere. They sort of pulled me. I couldn't take my eyes off them. Just to watch their skins. The way their necks twist, and sweat shines in the folds . . . I can't remember when it started. Mum reading to me about Prince who no one could ride, except one boy. Or the white horse in Revelations. "He that sat upon him was called Faithful and True. His eyes were as flames of fire, and he had a name written that no man knew but himself" . . . Words like reins. Stirrup. Flanks . . . "Dashing his spurs against his charger's flanks!" . . . Even the words made me feel -- . . . Years, I never told anyone. Mum wouldn't understand. She likes "Equitation". Bowler hats and jodhpurs! "My grandfather dressed for the horse," she says. What does that mean? The horse isn't dressed. It's the most naked thing you ever saw! More than a dog or a cat or anything. Even the most broken down old nag has got its life! To put a bowler on it is filthy! . . . Putting them through their paces! Bloody gymkhanas! . . . No one understands! . . . Except cowboys. They do. I wish I was a cowboy. They're free. They just swing up and then it's miles of grass . . . I bet all cowboys are orphans! . . . I bet they are! No one ever says to cowboys "Receive my meaning"! They wouldn't dare. Or "God" all the time. (Mimicking his mother.) "God sees you, Alan. God's got eyes everywhere --" (He stops abruptly.) I'm not doing any more! . . . I hate this! . . . You can whistle for anymore. I've had it!

DOES A TIGER WEAR A NECKTIE? by Don Petersen

Bickham -- 20 MALE -- SERIOUS

A troubled youth tells his psychiatrist what happened when he found his long lost father.

I wasn't ashamed! I was disgusted!! I was sick to my stomach. He made me puke . . . just like you do. That lousy sonofabitch! I spent my life thinkin' of him . . . lookin' for him. I dreamed for years of how him and me would get together some day. (Laughs, almost hysterically.) Get together! That's very funny. Him and me get together. (Pauses.) We talked all right. He told me stories . . . dirty little barber stories, and all the time I was diggin him. Then he starts askin' me questions. "Like the girls, huh? I bet they go for you in a big way," he says. Finally, out of a clear blue sky, he says, "You wanna see a picture of my wife and kid?" I don't know what the hell's comin off. I think, maybe . . . maybe he's talking about me and my mother, or somethin'. Maybe he's recognized me, for Chrissakes. "Sure," I says, "why not?" He goes to the drawer with this cat-eatin-shit grin all over his face . . . pretendin' all the time like it's a big secret or somethin'. He pulls out this picture, see, and brings it over and hands it to me. You wanna know what it was? (He laughs wildly . . . beginning to lose control.) After all those years . . . I meet my old man in a barber shop. He gives me a picture that I think is me . . . and my old lady. (Laughs bitterly.) You know what it was? A picture of some whorey lookin' blonde with her dress up to her ass and a baby sittin' on her lap. A baby . . . a baby boy, only it's a trick shot, see, like you'd buy on 42nd Street. A baby . . . a normal baby only the photographer . . . the photographer has dubbed in a yango. (A measuring gesture.) . . . a yango about that long! (Hysterically.) A baby with a tool that long and this two-bit blonde of a whore . . . I don't know what's happenin! I think it's gonna be a picture of me or somethin! I start shakin' all over. He's standin' there grinnin at me. He brings his hands down on my knee. "How ya like that for a kid," he says. "Takes after his old man, huh?" I drew a blank, see. I look at his face. I look at his grinning, slimy face. I pull the cloth off me and get up. "Hey," he says, "I ain't through yet. What are ya doin'?" I hit him. I hit him hard. He don't know nothin'. He goes flat on his ass . . . his nose busts like a ketchup bottle! I'm standin' over him . . . him whimperin' and cryin'. "Don't hit me, kid!" he shouts. "Take the money! It's in the drawer!" All the time he's tryin to hand me this key on a piece of string. I get down on top of him, and I hit him! I hit him and I hit him! Him screamin' for the bulls, and me hittin' him. (Softly.) Then, everything's quiet all of a sudden. I look down at him. . . and I know . . . I know just what I been waitin' for all my life. Whaddya looking at? Whaddya looking at, Doctor? You like the story? You got what you wanted. You got me off stuff. You cured me, Doctor, and now I belong to you.

BURIED CHILD by Sam Shepard

Vince -- 22 MALE -- SERIOUS

Vince explains to his girl friend why he can't run away from his family.

I was gonna run last night. I was gonna run and keep right on running. I drove all night. Clear to the Iowa border. The old man's two bucks sitting right on the seat beside me. It never stopped raining the whole time. Never stopped once. I could see myself in the windshield. My face. My eyes. I studied my face. Studied everything about it. As though I was looking at another man. As though I could see his whole race behind him. Like a mummy's face. I saw him dead and alive at the same time. In the same breath. In the windshield, I watched him breathe as though he was frozen in time. And every breath marked him. Marked him forever without him knowing. And then his face changed. His face became his father's face. And his father's face changed to his Grandfather's face. And it went on like that. Changing. Clear on back to faces I'd never seen before but still recognized. Still recognized the bones underneath. The eyes. The breath. The mouth. I followed my family clear into Iowa. Every last one. Straight into the Corn Belt and farther. Straight back as far as they'd take me. Then it all dissolved. Everything dissolved.

FIND YOUR WAY HOME by John Hopkins

Weston -- 23 MALE -- SERIOUS

Although desperately in love, a homosexual tries to hide his feelings for his lover.

You didn't leave home just to live with me? You didn't? I mean -- if you did -- hadn't you better think about it? How long do you think this is going to last? I won't be a comfort to you in your old age. There's nothing I hate more than old, painted queens -- and you're a whole lot older, love -- than I am. Twenty years? You haven't worn particularly well. You haven't taken care of yourself. You've lost your hair. You're getting soft. And smoking the way you do? How long will your heart put up with that? What d'you think -- I'm going to spend my life nursing an old man? Anyway, you'll soon get bored with me. I'm sort of stupid, when you get to know me. I'm not really meant to live with people, I've decided. Something happens in my head -- I expect . . . all sorts of idiotic things. It takes a lot of strength -- living with me -- and you're not very strong. I'm not sure you've got the strength to make it -- being queer. You meet a lot of funny people. You don't intend we sit here the rest of our lives -- the two of us -- together! Doesn't that sound sort of draggy? Another thing -- you could easily go back to girls. You've had a lot of practice. Since you can make it either way -- it's easier with girls -- easier to live -- you know? People don't look at you so funny -- with your arm around a girl -- even a fella -- old as you. (Silence.) You might go back to her. It's not impossible. You told each other some home truths tonight. Is that so bad? Could be the making of a great relationship. A little while -- you might fall in love. I'm an incurable romantic. (Harshly.) Why don't you get out of here? If you're going to sit there -- looking at me -- Christ! -- I can do without that. Accusing! What right have you -- accusing me. You think -- what? -- I failed you? All that stuff -- and you can only see -- I failed you? You get some bloody sort of standard and I'm supposed to live -- you're not here to help me -- love me -- keep them all away -- still -- I'm supposed . . . Because you condescend to love me -- not to live with me -- at the safe distance -- love me -- in your head -- where no one else can see -- not even me! Listen -- you failed me tonight. You let her scream at me.

You didn't stop her. You didn't try. I made you feel ashamed! I'm supposed to let her walk in here -- say what she likes -- scream at us? She called our making love -- filthy! You wouldn't stand up for yourself -- leave alone take care of me. I thought you were some special sort of thing. I thought you had decided to leave her, because your life with her was nothing. I thought -- you came here, because you loved me. I didn't understand -- you had this picture in your head -- some romantic dream of life with me -- and tenderness -- beauty! You can't come here -- running away from her -- using me. I won't survive, love -- when you run away from me. I've cut off from you -- for this moment -- free -- I can let you go. I want you to go. (Silence.) It would be easier. I could rest then -- be the person I am -- not have to try and be this person you have in your crazy head -- this -- innocent.

MY SWEET CHARLIE by David Westheimer

Charlie -- 20s, Black MALE -- SERIOUS

A black lawyer tells of his horrifying experience demonstrating for civil rights.

We assembled in what was left of the Mount Zion Baptist Church and marched to the business district. All very orderly. Ordinary. I was relieved, and disappointed. But when we got to the main street, all the people were waiting, lining the street on both sides, cursing, spitting, jeering. And every now and then a rock would come flying in among us. But we didn't even turn our heads. Jesus, it made me proud. Just to be with all those brave people. I was . . . I don't know, exalted. And then a white man hit me. Why me, I don't know. But he stepped off the curb and hit me. I hit him back. First time I'd hit anybody since I was a kid. They swarmed off the curb and grabbed me. Instead of going limp as I'd been briefed, I fought back. I kicked and bit and butted. Like a madman. And I broke loose. And I ran. God, how I ran. And they chased me. Yelling and screaming, and I knew if they caught me they'd kill me. Then I knew what it felt like to be a nigger. For the first time in my life I really knew. I ran until I couldn't run another step, but I kept running. I came to an alley and I ran in there. I heard one of them screaming, "Stop, you black nigger, you black bastard," and terrified as I was I wondered where he got the breath to scream. And when I reached the end of that dark alley and saw it was a dead-end I knew I was cornered. I shriveled up with fright and without even knowing how it happened I found myself curled up in a ball, down in the dirty. And then they were kicking me and yelling, "Nigger, get up, you nigger," and I suddenly realized it wasn't a mob, it was just one man, just one white man kicking me, and I got up out of the dirt. And I looked at him and it was his turn to be frightened. He snatched up a brick and tried to brain me with it but I got it away from him. (A pause.) I killed him.

THE SHADOW BOX by Michael Cristofer

Mark -- 20s MALE -- SERIOUS

His lover is dying of cancer, but Brian's ex-wife doesn't seem to care.

We are dying here, lady. That's what it's about. Brian looks at me and I can see it in his eyes. One stone slab smack in the face, the rug is coming out from under, the light is going out. You can do the pills and the syringes and the "let's play games" with the cotton swabs and x-rays, but it's not going to change it. You can wipe up the mucous and the blood and the piss and the excrement, you can burn the sheets and boil his clothes, but it's still there. You can smell it on him. It soaks into your hands when you touch him. It gets into your blood. It's stuck inside him, filling up inside his head, inside his skin, inside his mouth. You can taste it on him, you can swallow it and feel it inside your belly like a sewer. You wake up at night and you shake and you spit. You try to vomit it out of you. But you can't. It doesn't go away. It stays inside you. Inside every word, every touch, every move, every day, every night, it lies down with you and gets in between you. It's sick and putrid and soft and rotten and it is killing me.

And some of us have to watch it. Some of us have to live with it and clean up after it. I mean, you can waltz in and out of here like a fucking Christmas tree if you want, but some of us are staying. Some of us are here for the duration. And it is not easy.

OF THE FIELDS, LATELY by David French

Ben -- 20s MALE -- SERIOUS

A young man looks back at his painful relationship with his father.

It takes many incidents to build a wall between two men, brick by brick. Sometimes you're not aware of the building of the wall, and sometimes you are, though not always strong enough or willing enough to kick it down. It starts very early, as it did with my father and me, very early. And it becomes a pattern that is hard to break until the wall is made of sound brick and mortar, as strong as any my father ever built. Time would not level it. Only death.

I don't know if my father ever remembered one such incident. He never spoke of it to me, but I often thought it was the emotional corner-stone of the wall between us. He rushed out the door and down to the school-yard, the first game he had ever come to, and my mother put his supper in the oven, for later . . . I hadn't reminded my father of the game. I was afraid he'd show up and embarrass me. Twelve years old, and ashamed of my old man. Ashamed of his dialect, his dirty overalls, his bruised fingers with the fingernails lined with dirt, his teeth yellow as old ivory. Most of all, his lunchpail, that symbol of the working man. No, I wanted a doctor for a father. A lawyer. At least a fireman. Not a carpenter. That wasn't good enough . . . And at home my mother sat down to darn his socks and watch the oven . . . I remember stepping up to bat. The game was tied; it was the last of the ninth, with no one on base. Then I saw him sitting on the bench along third base. He grinned and waved, and gestured to the man beside him. But I pretended not to see him. I turned to face the pitcher. And angry at myself, I swung hard on the first pitch, there was a hollow crack, and the ball shot low over the short-stop's head for a double. Our next batter bunted and I made third. He was only a few feet away now, my father. But I still refused to acknowledge him. Instead, I stared hard at the catcher, pretending concentration. And when the next pitch bounced between the catcher's legs and home screen, I slid home to win the game. And there he was, jumping up and down, showing his teeth, excited as hell. And as the crowd broke up and our team stampeded out of the school-yard, cleats clicking and scraping blue sparks on the sidewalk, I looked back once through the wire fence and saw my father still sitting on the now-empty bench, alone, slumped over a little, staring at the cinders between his feet, just staring . . . I don't know how long he stayed there, maybe till dark, but I do know he never again came down to see me play. At home that night he never mentioned the game or being there. He just went to bed unusually early. . . .

P.S. YOUR CAT IS DEAD! by James Kirkwood

Vito -- 27 MALE -- SERIOUS

<u>A hustler tells what happened when he finally found someone he cared about.</u>

I just sort of fell into hustlin'. After begging for it, I meet someone wants it so bad, they pay me. Not only that, I get doused with affection. Right away, I figure I'm onto a winner; I figure I stumbled into my life's work. With men and women, don't make no difference. A lot of it was done for company. Serious, no cop-out. See, I'd just split with Dolores-from-Pasadena. Oh, man, great legs and melons, an ass like two duck eggs in a napkin -- but a face on her would back up a Chinese funeral! But sweet, very sweet! Anyhow, I was puttin' in time as a waiter between hook-ups in Santa Monica. Ben comes in with a party of eight one night. Well, I had banjo eyes for him right off, and I thought I was getting returns. Just to make sure -- and sorta open negotiations -- I dumped a cup of vichyssoise in his lap. Three days later, I'm takin' care of him and his house, on the beach, at Malibu, while he's beatin' his brains out designing this arts center. He was a big architect, Ben was, one of the <u>biggest</u>. He was at his drafting table all day. About five o'clock we took a swim, a trot on the beach, and there was this sunset goin' on, so spectacular it looked like a really rotten postcard. Unbelievable! We decided to make it. Well, it was wild. What with the sunset and all, it was wide-screen, stereo, panoramic sensurround! We zoomed up to Mars, shot over to Venus and hit Heaven head-on -- Bammo!

Rave reviews for everyone. Then, you know how you just lay there after a super-special one and try to uncross your eyes? After a while, I got up and I said, "I'll get a towel." "Okay," Ben said, "Get the little yellow one." There was this nice little yellow towel we kept in a drawer near the bed, but the laundry just come back and it was down the hall. I got up, went to the john, washed up, got the towel, and by the time I come back to the bedroom, the sunset had took a powder and the room was dark. I said his name, but he was asleep. So I figure to let him rest while I get dinner in the works. About seven o'clock, I fixed him a rum and diet cola and go back to the bedroom to wake him for the news on TV. "Hey, Ben," I said; no answer. I switched on the lights. (Pause.) He was lying on his back, those big brown eyes -- wide open. I -- I -- then I touched him . . . He was already cold. Would you ever imagine those would be the last two things two people would say, "I'll get a towel." "Okay, get the little yellow one."

VIEUX CARRE by Tennessee Williams

The Writer -- 28 MALE -- SERIOUS

Following a homosexual experience, a writer is visited by an apparition.

When I was alone in the room, the visitor having retreated beyond the plywood partition between his cubicle and mine, which was chalk white that turned ash-gray at night, not just he but everything visible was gone except for the lighter gray of the alcove with its window over Toulouse Street. An apparition came to me with the hypnotic effect of the painter's sandman special. It was in the form of an elderly female saint, of course. She materialized soundlessly. Her eyes fixed on me with a gentle questioning look which I came to remember as having belonged to my grandmother during her sieges of illness, when I used to go to her room and sit by her bed and want, so much, to say something or to put my hand over hers, but could do neither, knowing that if I did, I'd betray my feelings with tears that would trouble her more than her illness . . . Now it was she who stood next to my bed for a while. And as I drifted toward sleep, I wondered if she'd witnessed the encounter between the painter and me and what her attitude was toward such -- perversions? Of longing?

Nothing about her gave me any sign. The weightless hands clasping each other so loosely, the cool and believing gray eyes in the faint pearly face were as immobile as statuary. I felt that she neither blamed nor approved the encounter. No. Wait. She . . . seemed to lift one hand very, very slightly before my eyes closed with sleep. An almost invisible gesture of . . . forgiveness? . . . through understanding? . . . before she dissolved into sleep . . .

THE ECCENTRICITIES OF A NIGHTINGALE by Tennessee Williams

John -- late 20s, Southern MALE -- SERIOUS

A young doctor is surprised when his date suggests they go to a hotel.

I grew up in this town. Yes. I remember the place. It wasn't attractive, Miss Alma, you wouldn't like it. You might think that you would until you got there and then discover you didn't. The first time I went there was with one of those anonymous young ladies who get off the Cannonball Express at midnight and stand aimlessly around the entrance to the waiting room at the depot with one small suitcase like a small dog close to their slippers -- that first time I went there because she knew of the place . . . I made an excuse to slip away from the room, and I ran like a rabbit, ha, ha, I ran like a rabbit! -- I left a white linen jacket over a chair with a wallet containing eight dollars. Later, much later, I believe a year later, yes, the following summer -- I went back there again, and the grinning old colored porter handed me the white jacket. "A young lady left it for you, Mistuh Johnny, one time last summer," he told me. The wallet was still in the pocket, and in the wallet was a note from the lady. "Baby, I took five dollars to get me to Memphis." -- Ha ha ha -- signed "Alice" . . . Yes. Alice. She had a small nose with freckles which is probably still leading her into trouble as straight as a good bird dog will point at a partridge! Ha ha ha! -- No, Miss Alma, you wouldn't care for the place, and besides it's New Year's Eve and it will be crowded, there, and after all, you're not unknown in this town, you're the Nightingale of the Delta! Oh, they wouldn't be people you'd run into at church.

TODDY'S TAXI by Leonard Melfi

Toddy -- 30 MALE -- SERIOUS

A cab-driver tells his passengers about his unhappy marriage.

You might not believe it, but I'll tell you anyway. I met her on the subway a couple of years ago. I was sitting in a subway car, all by myself, reading the latest copy of Penthouse -- by the way, I hardly ever buy Penthouse anymore, only "Harder" and "Deeper" now, what great magazines they are! -- anyway, I was riding the subway one afternoon, when all of a sudden this beautiful-looking young thing -- she was nineteen, which, of course, I found out later on -- this beautiful gorgeous young creature began to pass out little folded-type cards and they were all different colors. When she came to me she half-smiled at me, and then I half-smiled back at her, and then she handed me a light blue, folding card, and I liked that right away because light blue is one of my favorite colors. The card said: "Hello! I am a deaf person, I am also a mute person. I am selling this deaf-mute education system card to make my living. Will you kindly buy one? Pay any price that you wish! Thank you!" And then the card instructed me to turn it over, which I did. On the back of it there was a drawn picture of a deaf-mute person showing me how it is to say "thanks" and how to say "good luck" by the way of the American Single-Hand Manual Alphabet For The Deaf and The Mute. Inside of the folded, light blue card were many little pictures with more instructions. "Hand alphabet used by the Deaf throughout the world. Easy to learn." (A pause.) And then there were hand diagrams indicating such words as: good, bad, perfect, chance, friend, o.k., right, no good, girl, thanks, boy, and, well, the last two were pictured diagrams for the words: sweetheart and marry. (A pause.) Her name was Alice and two months later we were both a sweetheart to each other, and in another two months we both decided to marry each other. (A pause.) It was heaven for awhile . . . Then, one day, and it really turned out to be a very bad day for me, I mean when you think about it now, well a real sort of strange miracle took place. My beautiful sexy little Alice, my brand-new beautiful young wife with her sexy-looking body was suddenly involved with an unexplained and very personal and very positive type of wild crazy miracle. Without warning: she was able to hear like the rest of us! Without warning: she was able to talk like the rest of us! (A pause.) It was a disaster for both of us. That's right, Gigi and Mimi: it was a horrible disaster for the two of us: my little Alice and me. She didn't like my voice. Can you believe it, ladies-of-the-night? (A pause.) And I didn't like her voice either: now that she could speak, well, I didn't want to hear her. It was awful. I wished that she were a mute again. (A pause.) We could not make love after that. She froze, and so did I. We were two frozen living creatures sleeping side-by-side in our frozen bedroom in our frozen bed in our frozen lives. (A pause.) It was a devastating thing. It was hell-on-earth. You see, we had been the perfect lovers. It was absolute perfection in that bed, in that bedroom, for my little Alice and me. (A pause.) Now, well, now, like I said before: it's hell-on-earth . . . a frozen hell in the middle of a frozen earth.

FANTASIES AT THE FRICK by Leonard Melfi

The Guard -- 30 MALE -- SERIOUS

A guard at the Frick Museum is on the verge of a mental breakdown.

We're about ready to close for the day. I don't know whether I like that or not. (A pause.) Listen, lady: will you listen to me? I didn't mean to frighten you before, what with my wanting to fight and kill and everything, I really didn't want to scare you, lady. I wasn't talking about ways to kill people before, I really wasn't. Take my word for it, okay? I was really talking about ways to kill myself, honest. Strangling myself by hanging myself. Shoving a kitchen carving knife into myself. Drowning in a very deep lake when a canoe is overturned. I can't swim, by the way. I learned almost everything, but I never learned how to swim. I come from the streets, remember? There's no need to swim because there's no place to really swim in the first place. (A nervous pause.) I meant that I would jump off the terrace from the twenty-fifth floor overlooking the East River. (Losing control.) I meant that I would throw myself in front of the fast traffic-ridden instant death before me! I MEANT IT ALL FOR ME! Not for you, nor for that man nor that woman, nor anybody else . . . especially NOT FOR YOU, LADY! (He is trying not to have a breakdown.) What do you want to know?! (Laughing rather strangely now.) Do you want to know where we're located?! Do you want to know the difference between our regular hours and our summer hours?! Do you want to know why we don't charge admission?! Restrictions?! (He laughs loud and rather out of control now.) Do you want to know about our restrictions?! Or do you want to know about just plain ole' restrictions in capital letters?! (Trembling.) Transportation?! TRANSPORTATION?! That's a new one! You want to know about transportation?! (He recites like a zombie, perhaps.) The Subway: IRT . . . the Lexington Avenue local . . . the Sixty-eighth Street station!" What about taking a bus?! "Buses . . . numbers one and four . . . southbound on Fifth Avenue and northbound on Madison Avenue!" Crosstown buses?! "Crosstown buses on Sixty-fifth Street . . . number M-7 . . . and Seventy-second Street . . . number 6 . . . !" Anything else, huh?! Anything else that you think you should know?! (He bows his head and cries.) I'm sorry, too . . . but did you really mean it when you wrote "I hate him" all over your bathroom mirror?! (He lifts his head.) Did you? Please tell me the truth. You don't have to lie to me, please . . . ?

THE ELEPHANT MAN by Bernard Pomerance

Treves -- 31, English MALE -- SERIOUS

A doctor is troubled by his inability to cure human misery.

Corsets. How about corsets? Here is a pamphlet I've written due mostly to the grotesque ailments I've seen caused by corsets. Fashion overrules me, of course. My patients do not unstrap themselves of corsets. Some cannot -- you know I have so little time in the week, I spend Sundays in the poor-wards; to keep up with work. Work being twenty-year-old women who look an abused fifty with worn-outedness; young men with appalling industrial conditions I turn out as soon as possible to return to their labors. Happily most of my patients are not poor. They are middle class. They overeat and drink so grossly, they destroy nature in themselves and all around them so fervidly, they will not last. Higher up, sir, above this middle class, I confront these same -- deformities -- bulged out by unlimited resources and the ruthlessness of privilege into the most scandalous dissipation yoked to the grossest of ignorance and constraint. I counsel against it where I can. I am ignored of course. Then, what, sir, could be troubling me? I am an extremely successful Englishman in a successful and respected England which informs me daily by the way it lives that it wants to die. I am in despair in fact. Science, observation, practice, deduction, having led me to these conclusions, can no longer serve as consolation. I apparently see things others don't.

ALL MY SONS by Arthur Miller

Chris -- 32 MALE -- SERIOUS

A disillusioned war veteran feels the war did nothing to make the world a better place.

You remember, overseas, I was in command of a company? Well, I lost them. Just about all. It takes a little time to toss that off. Because they weren't just men. For instance, one time it'd been raining several days and this kid came to me, and gave me his last pair of dry socks. Put them in my pocket. That's only a little thing . . . but . . . that's the kind of guys I had. They didn't die; they killed themselves for each other. I mean that exactly; a little more selfish and they'd 've been here today. And I got an idea -- watching them go down. Everything was being destroyed, see, but it seemed to me that one new thing was made. A kind of . . . responsibility. Man for man. You understand me? -- To show that, to bring that on to the earth again like some kind of a monument and everyone would feel it standing there, behind him, and it would make a difference to him. (Pause.) And then I came home and it was incredible. I . . . there was no meaning in it here; the whole thing to them was a kind of a -- bus accident. I went to work with Dad, and that rat-race again. I felt . . . what you said . . . ashamed somehow. Because nobody was changed at all. It seemed to make suckers out of a lot of guys. I felt wrong to be alive, to open the bank-book, to drive the new car, to see the new refrigerator. I mean you can take those things out of a war, but when you drive that car you've got to know that it came out of the love a man can have for a man, you've got to be a little better because of that. Otherwise what you have is really loot, and there's blood on it. I didn't want to take any of it. And I guess that included you.

HOSANNA by Michel Tremblay

Hosanna -- 30s MALE -- SERIOUS

A transvestite is not happy with his lifestyle.

They started with Bambi. Of course all her friends thought she was fabulous. I watched her. She was beautiful. Next, it was Candy's turn. Now Candy's a real dog, hein, but for once . . . she almost made it. They were cheering and whistling . . . The third Cleopatra was Carole. With a full length dress it was almost bearable, considering her legs don't grow in the same direction. After that . . . my turn. I don't know if you've ever heard a silence like that, Cuirette . . . I know I haven't. When Sandra called, or rather screamed my name, you'd have thought someone had cut off the sound. For a second I sat there nailed to my chair . . . I think I was already dead. Then I don't know who, but someone began to shout, "Hosanna, Hosanna, Hosanna,

Ho!" Then they all started banging their tables, yelling, "Hosanna, Hosanna. Come on, Liz, do your stuff!" You were laughing so hard, Cuirette. You were laughing so hard, it was you that made me decide to go up on that stage! So I got up . . . and I climbed the three steps, everyone shouting, "Hosanna, Hosanna," all around me . . . And right there, in the middle of the stage, with everyone laughing at me, and whistling, and calling me stupid names, I said to myself, "Cleopatra is a pile of shit! Elizabeth Taylor is a pile of shit! You asked for your pile of shit, Hosanna-de-Ste-Eustache. Well, here it is. Your big pile of shit!" Now listen, Cuirette, I wasn't Cleopatra anymore. I was Sampson, do you hear me? Sampson! And right there, I completely destroyed my papier mache set! Because you had completely destroyed my papier mache life. (Pause.) I never knew you all hated me so much . . . I'm a man, Raymond. If I ran out of there like that, tumbling down the stairs almost breaking my bloody neck, if I ran out, Raymond, it's because . . . I'm not a woman . . . And you're going to have to get used to that. . . .

BECKET OR THE HONOR OF GOD by Jean Anouilh

Becket -- 30s, English — MALE -- SERIOUS

The Archbishop of Canterbury finds he must choose God over his friend the King.

Yet it would be simple enough. Too simple perhaps. Saintliness is a temptation too. Oh, how difficult it is to get an answer from You, Lord! I was slow in praying to You, but I cannot believe that others, worthier than I, who have spent years asking You questions, have been better than myself at deciphering Your real intentions. I am only a beginner and I must make mistake after mistake, as I did in my Latin translations as a boy, when my riotous imagination made the old priest roar with laughter. But I cannot believe that one learns Your language as one learns any human tongue, by hard studying, with a dictionary, a grammar and a set of idioms. I am sure that to the hardened sinner, who drops to his knees for the first time and murmurs Your name, marveling, You tell him all Your secrets, straightaway, and that he understands. I have served You like a dilettante, surprised that I could still find my pleasure in Your service. And for a long time I was on my guard because of it. I could not believe this pleasure would bring me one step nearer You. I could not believe that the road could be a happy one. Their hair shirts, their fasting, their bells in the small hours summoning one to meet You, on the icy paving stones, in the sick misery of the poor ill-treated human animal -- I cannot believe that all these are anything but safeguards for the weak. In power and in luxury, and even in the pleasures of the flesh, I shall not cease to speak to You, I feel this now. You are the God of the rich man and the happy man too, Lord, and therein lies Your profound justice. You do not turn away Your eyes from the man who was given everything from birth. You have not abandoned him, alone in his ensnaring facility. And he may be Your true lost sheep. For Your scheme of things, which we mistakenly call Justice, is secret and profound and You plumb the hidden depths of poor men's puny frames as carefully as those of Kings. And beneath those outward differences, which blind us, but which to You are barely noticeable; beneath the diadem or the grime, You discern the same pride, the same vanity, the same petty, complacent preoccupation with oneself. Lord, I am certain now that You meant to tempt me with this hair shirt, object of so much vapid self-congratulation! this bare cell, this solitude, this absurdly endured winter-cold -- and the conveniences of prayer. It would be too easy to buy You like this, at so low a price. I shall leave this convent, where so many precautions hem You round. I shall take up the miter and the golden cape again, and the great silver cross, and I shall go back and fight in the place and with the weapons it has pleased You to give me. It has pleased You to make me Archbishop and to set me, like a solitary pawn, face to face with the King, upon the chessboard. I shall go back to my place, humbly, and let the world accuse me of pride, so that I may do what I believe is my life's work. For the rest, Your will be done. (He crosses himself.)

HOSANNA by Michel Tremblay

Cuirette -- late 30s MALE -- SERIOUS

A homosexual lashes out at his lover.

If you were a man, you'd act like a man, at least when you're alone. But no, when you're alone, you go behaving exactly like a woman. You never act like a man when you're anywhere near that goddamn mirror. And you sure as hell don't act like a man in bed . . . Especially there! . . . Yeah! In four years you haven't done one single thing in bed that would make me think you were a man, not one! You live like a woman, and you fuck like a woman. And ever since the lines started showing around your eyes and in the corners of your mouth, your pancake's getting thicker, just like a woman. You've even started wearing it to work, for Crissake. You can't go out of the house in daylight without putting half a pound of shit on your face. You're getting old, Hosanna. You're getting old the way a woman gets old . . . Fast! And it won't be long before you start getting all your crummy jokes about old queens right back in your face. It started tonight and let me tell you, that's only the beginning. Just a few more wrinkles on your lovely puss, and then, believe me, baby, the fur's gonna start flying. They'll be taking chunks out of you . . . The same treatment you've been giving them all these years. (Pause.) It's all over, Hosanna. After tonight, you're through playing the spring chicken. You hear me, Hosanna? After tonight you're through. And you want to know something really stupid? (Pause.) I love you, goddamn it. I love you!

PASSING GAME by Steve Tesich

Richard -- any age MALE -- SERIOUS

An actor tries to explain why he lied to his wife about his upbringing.

Because . . . because, because when I first saw her, Henry, she seemed like some wide-eyed angel who had plopped down from heaven to this cocktail party. There she stood . . . oh, she seemed so spanking sparkling new and unsoiled that I thought I'd love to be like that myself. That it could rub off. I wanted to make a fresh start and share with her something I had never shared with anyone else before. But there was nothing new I could tell her. So I . . . I started making up things . . . a love song to court her with. I created an orphanage where I grew up and populated it with these friends, Aldo and Tee-bone and the rest, who served as mouthpieces for words I was either ashamed or afraid to say on my own. Oh, they were lovely words, Henry. Full of poetry and pathos and unhesitating revelations . . . and I courted her with them. Had she been different she would have caught me at the start. But she was as trusting and openhearted as I made myself out to be . . . and the person she saw in me was far better than the person I really was. It was all based on a lie but in time, I thought, I could recreate myself and become as free and giving as that ghost of the orphanage I had created. It seemed possible. I tried but it got to be so hard. Keeping the ghosts alive. Keeping him fed. He turned into a vampire who sucked my soul and imagination dry just to keep going . . . and my life became like some ugly scar that I had to hide. I want to rip off my mask and tell her: Look, Julie, look . . . here I am. But I can't. It would almost be more cruel to do that than . . . I just can't.

T-SHIRTS by Robert Patrick

Marvin -- 40 MALE -- SERIOUS

Although rich and successful, a gay playwright is not satisfied.

I can't do anything about the way gay life is and I don't want to sour it for anybody that gets along in it. Christ, who am I to criticize the only world you've got? So you bang Greg and he gives you jobs on the building with him. Great. So you put out a little to the boys around the bar and it gets you drinks and identity and a certain amount of entree. Great. What's wrong with it? You weren't looking for true love or you wouldn't have gravitated to that corner. So kids come to New York -- or wherever -- and they wind up one more item in a permanent exhibition of drunks. Big deal. So what if some kid's values are so fucked up he can't hold a job for a week, but he's in his third smash year in the back room of the Anvil? Not my problem. Dammit. Why should you tell a kid like that he's systematically eroding his ability to function as a human being? What does he care? Who wants him to function as anything but a punchboard and an active element in the exciting, expanding gay market? Telling some kid who's having his first social success as a fist-fuckee that he's plugged into a conglomerate as heartless as Con Ed is as pointlessly cruel as telling a girl from the Bronx that Binaca causes cancer! So what if his cock is always soft from chemicals -- like Wonder Bread? Wonder Bread sells! He sells! He sells seashells by the seashore on Fire Island while he's blowin' his boss to get his first article into _Opera News_! So he gets the heebie-jeebies from Phebe's and CeebeeGeebee's and his heavy leather isn't heavy enough to stop his fits of shaking? Well, hell, what would there be for an American to do if he _did_ grow up? There is counseling, there are tranquilizers, there's est and Sun Myung Moon and the Church of the Beloved Disciple and other forms of no-fault philosophy, Gail Sheehy live forever, and there's always the statistics on impotence, alcoholism, and suicide to make you feel you're not in this alone. Long-lasting relationships and thoughtful productive citizens don't do a damn thing for the disco business anyway. Stop me, huh? . . . Well, don't believe a word of it, big breeches. If I had the slightest chance of gettin in on any of it, you wouldn't hear a peep from me! The only reason I'm reactionary is because I get no reactions. My sex life has been limited to desperate drunks, indifferent junkies, catch-as-catch-can in the darkest corners of the baths, and other forms of bestiality with people! Have fun. Sell what you've got to sell! Get what you can for it! So what if sex has become nothing but a product of moral frustration? Even if it is a fault, it's not yours! When a society's only values are good looks and money, sooner or later people are going to wind up exchanging the one for the other! Gay life is great. Gay life is paradise. It's just that paradise lost . . . me. (_He stands, a tragic figure, head bowed, fists clenched._)

FIND YOUR WAY HOME by John Hopkins

Harrison -- 47 MALE -- SERIOUS

A homosexual tries to explain to his lover why he deserted him.

(_Quietly._) I ran away, Julie -- mostly from myself. (_Silence._) If what you are disgusts you -- the man you are -- how can you live with any hope of being -- knowing -- happiness -- or peace? No -- you can only punish -- prove to yourself -- yes -- I am disgusting. There is some satisfaction . . . (_Silence._) I thought it was meant. I thought -- this is the man you are -- the life you've made -- and now -- accept it. What did you expect? What right have you -- has anyone! -- expecting the life they want -- perhaps -- think they deserve? (_Smiling._) I caught myself thinking -- if I'm so special -- and I am! -- how is it no one sees? I lived ten years -- and every day lies, deceit -- and endless little insincerities. I had affaires -- pathetic, cruel affaires. Women at first -- then girls -- because the women asked -- expected -- more than I could give them -- time and consideration -- and the girls -- they didn't take it seriously. They had the time to pass -- and passing it with me -- it wasn't painful -- sometimes boring, I suppose -- but there were compensations. I always bought them presents -- and they didn't know I wasn't really there -- I wasn't ever there. Any more -- I think -- than Jackie knew. There was excitement -- running from bed to bed -- a sense of power -- able to have -- no -- not any woman I might choose -- but I was careful and I chose without much risk they would refuse and so -- could tell myself -- with anyone I chose. (Silence.) Much more important -- sleeping with strangers -- I could make an answer to the question -- why -- with my wife -- with Jackie -- why don't I feel desire -- why can't I make myself enjoy -- why? -- and in all the other beds -- thinking of her -- I could tell myself -- if anyone's at fault, it surely isn't me. (Silence.) I played so many games with truth I lost all sense of honesty. Business trips -- late dinners -- entertaining guests in town -- visiting executives -- I had a madness in my head. I never told the truth to anyone -- (Silence.) Once -- I arranged an evening on my own -- with all the same elaborate mechanism -- time to think -- time -- to step back and look at this whole distorted pattern of reality. I found -- there was no one in my life I trusted. No one I could let come close -- no one could even understand -- no one who knew the simple basic fact -- my life -- everything -- was part of this same lie -- this slight -- but central! -- divergence from the truth. I had contrived an absolute aloneness for myself. Why did I go away? You have to understand, love -- at that time -- truthfully, I thought -- that was the life I wanted -- and most of the time -- enjoyed it -- It was a sort of death -- but locked inside -- keeping my head down and my eyes closed -- I was happy -- and why not! What's so much better here? -- out here! -- and I'm not happy -- more alone -- and all the time -- aware! (Silence.) I did come here tonight -- thinking we could make love -- and right away -- before we talked -- before anything! -- make love. That was the fantasy -- blanking out thought -- and all consideration -- just -- the memory of every night we spent here.

COLD STORAGE by Ronald Ribman

Landau -- mid 40s MALE -- SERIOUS

A Jew remembers how he, but not his family, survived Nazi Germany.

My father found a man . . . Luis Boscan. And for money . . . I guess everything my father had left . . . he took care of me. His wife used to tell me that they would have taken my sister, too, but my mother was afraid to let her go . . . she was just a baby . . . it was a choice . . . It wasn't a matter of money . . . my mother made a choice. I . . . um . . . Anyway, they were nice people. I still write to them. Sometimes they write to me. They like to tell me about the time they met my father . . . where it was, what the day was like, what he was wearing . . . they always seem to find something new, some little detail . . . I . . . I don't like talking about the Boscans. My life is a history of the Boscans! Their sons, and the businesses their sons went into! Their daughters and who they married! Their grandchildren!

My life has a history that has nothing to do with the Boscans! It had a beginning! It had people in it! It had . . . It had . . . what did it have? What? I would sit by a window thinking the day would come when my father would walk around the corner of that alley again . . . my mother, my sister . . . my sister . . . Oh God. How many years did I sit by that window wishing they had saved her instead of me. Waiting! Waiting! Just like the rest of them. Waiting for passports that never arrived, waiting for boats that would take us out of there, waiting at the embassies, the British, the American, waiting to reach invisible people, diplomats who could save anyone, if only you could touch them -- but you couldn't, because they hid themselves down corridors no refugee could enter, behind doors no Jew could open! A world died trying to touch these faceless people who had no pity, while I sat by a window -- waiting!

EQUUS by Peter Shaffer

Dysart -- mid 40s, English MALE -- SERIOUS

Having dealt with a boy who blinded 6 horses, a psychiatrist questions the nature of his work.

(Crying out.) All right! I'll take it away! He'll be delivered from madness. What then? He'll feel himself acceptable! What then? Do you think feelings like his can be simply re-attached, like plasters? Stuck on to other objects we select? Look at him! . . . My desire might be to make this boy an ardent husband -- a caring citizen -- a worshipper of abstract and unifying God. My achievement, however, is more likely to make a ghost! . . . Let me tell you exactly what I'm going to do to him! I'll heal the rash on his body. I'll erase the welts cut into his mind by flying manes. When that's done, I'll set him on a nice mini-scooter and send him puttering off into the Normal world where animals are treated properly: made extinct, or put into servitude, or tethered all their lives in dim light, just to feed it! I'll give him the good Normal world where we're tethered beside them -- blinking our nights away in a non-stop drench of cathode-ray over our shrivelling heads! I'll take away his Field of Ha Ha, and give him Normal places for his ecstasy -- multi-lane highways driven through the guts of cities, extinguishing Place altogether, even the idea of Place! He'll trot on his metal pony tamely through the concrete evening -- and one thing I promise you: he will never touch hide again! With any luck his private parts will come to feel as plastic to him as the products of the factory to which he will almost certainly be sent. Who knows? He may even come to find sex funny. Smirky funny. Bit of grunt funny. Trampled and furtive and entirely in control. Hopefully, he'll feel nothing at his fork but Approved Flesh. I doubt, however, with much passion! . . . Passion, you see, can be destroyed by a doctor. It cannot be created. . . . You won't gallop any more, Alan. Horses will be quite safe. You'll save your pennies every week, till you can change that scooter in for a car, and put the odd fifty P on the gee-gees, quite forgetting that they were ever anything more to you than bearers of little profits and little losses. You will, however, be without pain. More or less completely without pain. (Pause.) And now for me it never stops: that voice of Equus out of the cave -- 'Why Me? . . . Why Me? . . . Account for Me!' . . . All right -- I surrender! I say it! . . . In an ultimate sense I cannot know what I do in this place -- yet I do ultimate things. Essentially I cannot know what I do -- yet I do essential things. Irreversible, terminal things. I stand in the dark with a pick in my hand, striking at heads! I need -- more desperately than my children need me -- a way of seeing in the dark. What way is this? . . . What dark is this? . . . I cannot call it ordained of God: I can't get that far. I will however pay it so much homage. There is now, in my mouth, this sharp chain. And it never comes out.

ALL MY SONS by Arthur Miller

Keller -- late 50s MALE -- SERIOUS

A manufacturer tries to defend to his son his decision to sell defective plane parts to the Air Force.

Exactly what's the matter? What's the matter? You got too much money? Is that what bothers you? If you can't get used to it, then throw it away. You hear me? Take every cent and give it to charity, throw it in the sewer. Does that settle it? In the sewer, that's all. You think I'm kidding? I'm tellin' you what to do, if it's dirty then burn it. It's your money, that's not my money. I'm a dead man, I'm an old dead man, nothing's mine. Well, talk to me! -- what do you want to do! What should I want to do? Jail? You want me to go to jail? If you want me to go, say so! Is that where I belong? -- then tell me so! (Slight pause.) What's the matter, why can't you tell me? (Furiously.) You say everything else to me, say that! (Slight pause.) I'll tell you why you can't say it. Because you know I don't belong there. Because you know! (With growing emphasis and passion, and a persistent tone of desperation.) Who worked for nothin' in that war? When they work for nothin', I'll work for nothin'. Did they ship a gun or a truck outa Detroit before they got their price? Is that clean? It's dollars and cents, nickels and dimes; war and peace, it's nickels and dimes, what's clean? Half the Goddamn country is gotta go if I go! That's why you can't tell me.

I WAS DANCING by Edwin O'Connor

Daniel -- 70s MALE -- SERIOUS

An old man tries to defend his lifestyle to his son.

I never said I was a saint. I never said I did no wrong. All right. I left your mother. I left you. I didn't leave you broke, and I didn't let you starve. But I did leave you. And that was wrong. It was a bad thing to do. But you're young, Tom. You're a smart boy, but you're young, and maybe you don't understand that there's not just bad things and good things. But sometimes a bad thing might not be so bad, if only you could explain it a little. But I can't explain this one to you, because you wouldn't understand any more than your mother did. She never understood me: the kind of man I was, the kind of thing I did. Once I tried to explain to her that a man like myself, an actor, a fellow on the stage, was a little different from other people, and that maybe he had to be. She laughed. You called me a dancing man, Tom. Well, that's what I am. That's what I always was. I was always a dancing man. All the years I danced, I never got tired of it or any part of it. You'll never understand this in a million years, Tom, no more than your mother did, but to come running out on the stage, you know, and hear everybody in the place start to yell and clap their hands as soon as they catch sight of you -- oh, it's like bombs going off and the Fourth of July all rolled into one, and it's all for you! Oh, I tell you, you don't forget a thing like that, Tom! And you never, never, never, get tired of it. Oh yes, I always loved the dancing! . . . Well . . . you don't understand. Why should you? I only told you this because . . . well, no matter. All I want to say now is I did wrong. But I didn't mean to harm you. I never meant that for a single second of my life. And if I did you any harm, all I want to say is I'm sorry.

LOVERS by Brian Friel

Joe -- 17, Irish MALE -- SERIO-COMIC

A young man is puzzled by his relationship with his father.

Your father, Mag, my God, he's such a fine man. And your mother -- I mean she's such a fine woman. I remember -- oh, I was only a boy at the time -- I remember seeing them walking together out the Dublin Road; And I thought they were so -- you know -- so dignified looking. I'd like to be like him. God, such a fine man. And so friendly to everyone. You're lucky to have parents like that. . . . My aul fella -- lifting the dole on a Friday -- that's what he lives for. She laughs and calls him her man Friday; but I don't know how she can laugh at it. And to listen to him talking -- cripes, you'd think he was bloody Solomon. How he can sit on his backside and watch her go out every morning with her apron wrapped in a newspaper under her arm -- Honest to God, I don't know how he does it. I said it to her once, you know; called him a loafer or something. And you should have seen her face! I thought she was going to hit me! "Don't you ever -- ever -- say the likes of that again. You'll never be half the man he is." Loyalty, I suppose; 'cause when you're that age, you hardly -- you know -- really love your husband or wife any more. . . . Did I ever tell you what he does when there's no racing? He has this tin trunk under his bed; he keeps all my old school reports in it. And he sits up there in the cold and takes out the trunk and pores over all those old papers -- term reports and all, away back to my primary school days! Real nut! I know damn well when he's at it 'cause I can hear the noise of the trunk on the lino. And once when I went into the room he tried to stuff all the papers out of sight. Strange, too, isn't it . . . You know, we never speak at all, except maybe "Is the tea ready?" or "Bring in some coal." . . . Sitting up there in that freezing attic, going over my old marks . . . Maybe when I'm older, maybe we'll go to football matches together, like Peadar Donnelly and his aul fella . . . I don't like football matches but he does; and we wouldn't have to speak to each other -- except going and coming back. . . .

PHILADELPHIA, HERE I COME by Brian Friel

Private -- 20s, Irish MALE -- SERIO-COMIC

A young man ponders his relationship with his father.

When you're curled up in your wee cot, Screwballs, do you dream? Do you ever dream of the past, Screwballs, of that wintry morning in Bailtefree, and the three days in Bundoran? . . . and of the young, gay girl from beyond the mountains who sometimes cried herself to sleep? (Softly, nervously, with growing excitement.) God -- maybe -- Screwballs -- behind those dead eyes and that flat face are there memories of precious moments in the past? My God, have I been unfair to you? Is it possible that you have hoarded in the back of that mind of yours -- do you remember -- it was an afternoon in May -- oh, fifteen years ago -- I don't remember every detail but some things are as vivid as can be: the boat was blue and the paint was peeling and there was an empty cigarette packet floating in the water at the bottom between two trout and the left rowlock kept slipping and you had given me your hat and had put your jacket round my shoulders because there had been a shower of rain. And you had the rod in your left hand -- I can see the cork nibbled away from the butt of the rod -- and maybe we had been chatting -- I don't remember -- it doesn't matter -- but between us at that moment there was this great happiness, this great joy -- you must have felt it too -- it was so much richer than a content -- it was a great, great happiness, and active, bubbling joy -- although nothing was being said -- just the two of us fishing on a lake on a showery day -- and young as I was I felt, I knew, that this was precious, and your hat was soft on the top of my ears -- I can feel it -- and I shrank down into your coat -- and then, then for no reason at all except that you were happy too, you began to sing: (Sings.)

All round my hat I'll wear a green coloured ribbono,
All round my hat for a twelve month and a day.
And if anybody asks me the reason why I wear it,
It's all because my true love is far, far away.

SAY GOODNIGHT, GRACIE by Ralph Pape

Steve -- late 20s MALE -- SERIO-COMIC

Steve tells of the ending of a relationship.

Right, right -- it was a pure Hollywood ending. I mean, our last day together. The final scene. In the rain, no less. And her telling me with tears in her eyes that I was living in this fantasy world. Right? Now, you have to picture this: this rain, the two of us standing together on the sidewalk, not moving, just looking at each other, in close-ups, the camera cutting back and forth between our faces. This warm Spring rain . . . (He's having fun, still in control, the Movie Director -- but as he continues, it is clear that the memory controls him.) And then she said goodbye, and turned, and walked away. And as I watched her, I could feel the camera pulling back for a long shot . . . and I felt her about to become a memory and I remembered watching her walking with her friends, it was like a slow-motion flashback you know, in the rain, or singing, the wind blowing her hair . . . and I ran after her and I held her shoulders and . . . I turned her around and I said to her: the very first time I saw you, you were walking in the rain, I saw you from a window in the library, and you were soaked and you looked so helpless, the leaves were all over you, and even though I didn't know who you were, I wanted to take off my coat and put it around you, which you would never have let me do, but I thought at that moment . . . that it would have been possible not to be afraid of anything . . . if only I could place my coat around someone I loved . . . and pretend that I could protect her . . . I just wanted to tell you that . . .

LEMON SKY by Lanford Wilson

Alan -- 29 MALE -- SERIO-COMIC

A writer introduces his story to the audience.

I've been trying to tell this story, to get it down, for a long time, for a number of years, seven years at least -- closer to ten. I've had the title, I've had some of the scenes a dozen times, a dozen different ways, different starts. The times I've told it to friends as something I wanted to do I've come home and tried to get it down -- get to work on it -- but the characters, the people ignored the damn story and talked about whatever they darn well pleased and wouldn't have any part of what I wanted them to say. They sat down to coffee or some damn thing. The trouble was I wanted not to be the big deal, the hero, because I wasn't. No one was. Or how do I know who was? If it happened this way or that, who knows? But dad -- my dad -- (Quickly.) If it's all autobiographical, so, I'm sorry, there it is; what can I tell you -- But how can I write about dad? Tell him. I knew him, lived with him, that I can remember, for six months. (Quickly.) I always say I lived in California for two years because it sounds more romantic. Bumming around the beach a couple of years, on the coast, it sounds great. Six months is like you didn't fit in. Like why bother. Like restlessness. The title because -- I don't know -- it had something to do with the state. California. I mean, the nut fringe; first Brown, then Reagan and -- who knows what they'll come up -- (Breaking off, returning to the thought above.) But finally I said, so if you're a hero; if you can't admit that you were really as big a bastard as everybody else -- If you can't admit that, then for God's sake let it stay! And the fact that you can't will say more about you than if you could. Leave it be! My father, what do I know about him. If he's nothing, I mean But nothing! Then the fact that he comes off the short end of the stick shows something. From that you know that there's more there. You know? Leave it! Do it. Straight. Get it down, let it get down and let it tell itself and mirror, by what you couldn't say -- what was really there.

JOE EGG by Peter Nichols

Bri -- 33, English MALE -- SERIO-COMIC

The father of a spastic child explains his relationship to his wife.

Hear that noise? That's Mummy in the bedroom. Probably taken her dress off now. Might be putting her stockings on. Even changing entirely. Every stitch. Naked, looking at herself in the glass, thinking have I kept my figure? (Pause. Dwells on image.) But I'm not running up those stairs three at a time and falling into the bedroom and cringing on the carpet begging her not to go. No fear! I've done all I can without total loss of dignity. I might have known once I got her started on amateur theatricals she'd turn up at every bloody practice. Terrible sense of duty, your mum. What am I doing talking to you? (Talks to audience.) Might as well be talking to the wall. No, but she is a wonderful woman, my wife. That girl upstairs. In the bedroom, off in the wings, wherever she is. No, seriously. A truly integrated person. Very rare, that is, as you know. Give you an example: she's disturbed by anything, she's not just mentally upset about it, not only miserable, no, she actually grows ill. Boils, backache, vomiting. Not pretence. Real sickness. She works as a whole, not in parts. Unlike me, for instance, I'm Instant Man. Get one for Christmas, endless fun. I'm made up as I go along from old lengths of string, fag-ends . . . magazine cuttings, film-clips . . . all stuck together with wodges of last week's school dinner. What I mean, she couldn't pretend a passion she doesn't feel. Whereas I can't sustain a passion to the end of the sentence. I start to cry -- aaaoooow! Then I think: are you mad? Who do you think you are, God? And things go clang and wheels fall off and people get hurt -- terrible. You must have felt like this -- catching yourself in the mirror hamming away. Or somebody says. "My wife's just been run over," and you want to burst out laughing. Well, you may say, why not -- if that's the way you feel? But other people don't like it. So I pretend. You saw me pretend with Sheila. I try to guess which emotions appeal to her and then I sink my teeth in. I don't let go until they're bone-dry. Like with Joe there -- (Waves to her.) All right, are you? Good. I felt all doomy at first but -- well -- ten years! I just go through the motions now. Sheila -- how shall I put it in a way that will prevent a sudden stampede to the exit-doors? Sheila -- embraces all living things. She really does. She's simple, so simple she's bound to win in the end. She's a sane enough person to be able to embrace all living creatures. She sits there embracing all live things. I get my hug somewhere between the budgerigar and the stick-insect. Which is the reason for all this smutty talk. Calling attention to myself to make sure I get more than my share. Otherwise I'd have to settle for eyes-front-hands-on-heads and a therapeutic bash once in a blue moon. And I'm too young to die, I tell you!

THE SEA HORSE by Edward J. Moore

Harry -- 30s MALE -- SERIO-COMIC

In a roundabout way, a seaman proposes to his girl friend.

Awhile back . . . I get relieved off the midwatch, and I come topside out of that stinking hot engine room . . . I open the hatch . . . and I feel strange . . . (Laughs.) It's hard to explain . . . I remember the sea was so calm that night, I mean, not a ripple. It doesn't happen too often, the sight is unbelievable if you've never seen it before . . . can you imagine . . . an ocean, an ocean! As far as you can see, that looks like a sheet of glass, like you could walk out on it. The moon up full . . . the sky, not a cloud . . . just all freckled up, with tiny little diamonds . . . all the years I been steaming I never seen anything like it . . . not like that night . . . well, I walked aft and I sat down on number four davit . . . I could feel the screw humming under me . . . (Makes humming noise.) and I sat there, watching our wake cutting through this glazed sheet of ice . . . And I started thinking of a kid . . . ya see. I imagined myself sitting there with a little boy next to me . . . and he was my son . . . and it was so real I could see him. He had a tiny pair of non-skids on, and khakis, and a little striped sweater, I remember it was blue. And he had on one of my old watch caps, it was cut down and pulled over his ears to keep out the night cold. And he was sitting on a cushion next to me and I had my arm around him and I was tellin' him all about the sea and everything . . . you know I must have sat there for over an hour just talkin' to him . . . and that's when I started making my plans . . . ya see, I want that kid! And I want my own boat, that's why it's so important I talk to Hank, so I don't have to be away from him so long. And I'd like to get an old beat-up house somewhere, that way it would be cheap, and I could fix it up. And when he gets old enough, I want him to go out with me . . . on the boat, and his old man will teach him how to be the best damn little salt! (Smiles.) And he'll have a great mom! (A moment.) Well . . . what do ya think?

RED ROVER, RED ROVER by Oliver Hailey

Joe -- 40s MALE -- SERIO-COMIC

A middle-aged man remembers a children's game that brought him joy.

You know the only time I was ever really happy and knew it -- at the time? That's the trick, you know -- reading the meter as it runs. When I was a kid, we used to play a game called Red Rover, Red Rover. We'd lock arms and line up on opposite sides. Then we'd call out to the other team, "Red Rover, Red Rover, let Eddie come over." Or Nell. Or Leigh. Or Harris. (Thoughtful beat -- then finally.) Or Vic. If they couldn't crash through the line -- if our arms held -- then they had to join our team. You want to know when I was happiest? When every kid on the street was holding hands in one long line -- all of us together, arms locked -- the length of the block. Sometimes I'd even pretend I was going to lead them into my house. To spend the night. To spend all the nights. I don't care how much coffee Vic spills on me -- or how lousy the mattress is -- this is a terrific night. Toilets flushing, doors opening, beds squeaking -- all over the house. I'll sleep like a baby.

WHO'S AFRAID OF VIRGINIA WOOLF? by Edward Albee

George -- 46 MALE -- SERIO-COMIC

A professor remembers a moment from his youth.

When I was sixteen and going to prep school, during the Punic Wars, a bunch of us used to go into New York on the first day of vacations, before we fanned out to our homes, and in the evening this bunch of us used to go to this gin mill owned by the gangster-father of one of us -- for this was during the Great Experiment, or Prohibition, as it is more frequently called, and it was a bad time for the liquor lobby, but a fine time for the crooks and the cops -- and we would go to this gin mill, and we would drink with the grown-ups and listen to the jazz. And one time, in the bunch of us, there was this boy who was fifteen, and he had killed his mother with a shotgun some years before -- accidentally, completely accidentally, without even an unconscious motivation, I have no doubt, no doubt at all -- and this one evening this boy went with us, and we ordered our drinks, and when it came his turn he said, I'll have bergin . . . give me some bergin, please . . . bergin and water. Well, we all laughed . . . he was blond and he had the face of a cherub, and we all laughed, and his cheeks went red and the color rose in his neck, and the assistant crook who had taken our order told people at the next table what the boy had said, and then they laughed, and then more people were told and the laughter grew, and more people and more laughter, and no one was laughing more than us, and none of us more than the boy who had shot his mother. And soon, everyone in the gin mill knew what the laughter was about, and everyone started ordering bergin, and laughing when they ordered it. And soon, of course, the laughter became less general, but it did not subside, entirely, for a very long time, for always at this table or that someone would order bergin and a new area of laughter would rise. We drank free that night, and we were brought champagne by the management, by the gangster-father of one of us. And, of course, we suffered the next day, each of us, alone, on his train, away from New York, each of us with a grown-up's hangover . . . but it was the grandest day of my . . . youth.